Teacher's Notes

Mr. Bach Comes to Call

Based on the original work
by Martin and Karen Lavut

Teacher's Notes written
by Susan Hammond

To Sarah and Katie,
who inspired this series

Published by The Children's Group Inc.
1400 Bayly Street, Suite 7
Pickering, Ontario, Canada L1W 3R2
For a complete catalogue, please call 1-800-757-8372
or e-mail moreinfo@childrensgroup.com
Visit us online at http://www.childrensgroup.com

Printed in Canada

CONTENTS

Letter to Teachers

Children love the possibility of time travel, whether reliving history or facing an uncharted future. While most of the Classical Kids series look backwards in time, *Mr. Bach Comes to Call* goes forward into our century where the composer visits a nine-year-old girl named Elizabeth. As she struggles with his Minuet in G, Bach charmingly describes his life with 20 children, family picnics, love of the organ, time spent in jail and his belief that:

"Every single time my music is being played... I am there, too."

Almost every music student cuts his or her teeth on Bach's minuets, inventions and fugues. Indeed, so many musicians begin their day playing Bach that we feel compelled to ask what draws them there? Bach would answer humbly:

"All my music I wrote for God..."

There is something spacious, something eternal, in every note Bach wrote. At the same time, his music can be full of playfulness, something we try to capture in the "Adventure in Music." On this recording, you will hear "All Around the Mulberry Bush" played forward, upside down and on top of itself, before Elizabeth's opening minuet asserts itself along with a gigue and "In Dulce Jubilo."

Unlike the letters of Mozart and Tchaikovsky, Bach's letters reveal little of his personality. Instead we must turn to his occasional poems, his Coffee Cantata, his music and his hectic child-filled life, to discover a tireless composer full of humor, zest and love of life. Children respond to Bach's approachable, sardonic manner as he describes his life composing enough music to occupy a modern-day copyist for 60 years! As the biologist Lewis Thomas commented on seeing the list of music sent into space aboard *Voyager:*

"We would have sent all the works of Johann Sebastian Bach, but that would have been bragging!"

Whether you have an extensive background in music or none at all, in these Teacher's Notes you will find more than 70 suggestions ranging broadly across the integrated curriculum: personal biography, social history, geography, science, creative writing, drama, dance, art and music. Here, your library research is collected in one place, along with many classroom activity ideas.

Many teachers have concerns about using audio productions in the classroom where the "fidget factor" cannot be tamed by "things to look at." Yet listening to recordings in class, like reading aloud, can encourage children to create whole worlds in their imaginations. This creative listening is one of childhood's greatest gifts, and is an essential skill for later life.

Let us give our children a window on earlier times, accompanied by glorious music, enticing drama and some profound themes.

Susan Hammond

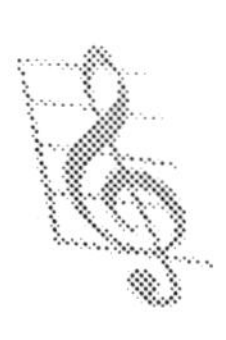

How This Book Is Organized

Classical Kids recordings have been used in K–9 classes, but are most suitable for Grades K to 6. We have ranked the activities according to grade level with the symbols below. The icon applies to all the activities in the section, unless otherwise indicated. In the Exploring the Music sections, the icon also includes a number indicating the appropriate National Standard for Arts Education (see page 5).

 K–2 3–4  5–6  3–6  All

Presenting the Recording

This recording can be presented in its entirety (approximately 45 minutes), in two halves or in the six scenes outlined here. Each scene is identified in terms of tape time elapsed, CD track numbers and beginning and ending dialogue. You will find in these Teacher's Notes:

Getting ready: Questions and activities for use before the recording

Scene-by-scene suggestions: For use during the recording
- The story
- Music used in the scene
- Interesting background facts
- Discussion and activity suggestions
- Suggestions for exploring the music

Follow-up: Questions and activities for use after the recording
- Charts: Themes and skills, and a 10-day lesson plan
- Student's worksheet

Music in the Integrated Curriculum

Although Classical Kids recordings can be enjoyed as musical stories, our aim is to move children from being passive listeners to active participants: to engage their imaginations, to offer new skills and knowledge, to stimulate higher-order thinking skills and, finally, to give every teacher the tools to build a rich learning environment. These Teacher's Notes present more than 70 facts and thought-provoking questions to move beyond music into an integrated curriculum of social studies, creative writing, math, sciences and the other arts.

Our intent is to provide both specialists and general classroom teachers with engaging materials that expand their students' knowledge of music and times past. Instead of presenting a basal text of sequential musical skills, Classical Kids urges teachers and their students to "play with" musical concepts, to develop an interpretive vocabulary, to sing or play classical melodies on simple classroom instruments, to write lyrics, even to venture into composition. Children find it difficult to work in a vacuum, so let these recordings serve as a model, captivating young listeners with a moving story and then motivating them to acquire new facts and skills. Put these recordings in your classroom library for repeated listening.

Classical Kids and Children with Special Needs

Classical Kids recordings do not talk down to children. Our challenge here has been to design concrete activities that are sufficiently broadly based to inspire and involve children with special needs.

Teachers of children with learning disabilities often use the activities designed for younger classes, or allow more time for tasks: retell the story, dance, draw, sing or clap. Those teaching children with physical disabilities concentrate on singing, storyboarding, drawing or discussing events from the past. Teachers of children who are deaf or hard of hearing can tell the compelling story of Beethoven's triumph over deafness in *Beethoven Lives Upstairs*.

ESL students benefit from recordings that use well-spoken English to promote oral comprehension. Singing and writing lyrics are also wonderful ways to learn a second language. Classical Kids materials are available in other languages. Illustrated books of *Beethoven Lives Upstairs* and *Tchaikovsky Discovers America* are available in Spanish, and recordings of *Beethoven Lives Upstairs* and *Vivaldi's Ring of Mystery* are available in French.

The Teacher's Notes in this series encourage gifted students to write variations, study rondo structure, venture into European history and write time-travel stories with shifting points of view.

To all students, we encourage you to ask: "Who would want to do the possible all your life? The *impossible* — that's exciting!"

Assessment

Assessment in the arts is always difficult, often subjective, yet ultimately essential to spur excellence. Depending on what you hope to achieve with your arts program, you can test students individually or in groups, orally or on paper, for skills or understandings. These Notes encourage children to form their own questions, define tasks, discover research strategies, justify interpretations and then create a final product. Each of these stages can be assessed by the teacher. A sample student worksheet is included at the end of this book.

Observe and assess your students not only on final results but also on the care taken with the process. We encourage specialists to move beyond traditional music skills into cultural history, creative writing, research projects, time lines, story boards, set designs, murals or dance. Conversely, general classroom teachers are urged to try musical activities not necessarily based on playing proficiency. These listening and interpretive skills are important for music and for life in general.

Exploring the Music with Classical Kids

The suggested activities in the Exploring the Music sections are coded by number to reflect how they fulfill the U.S. National Standards for Arts Education.

1. *Singing, alone and with others, a varied repertoire of music.* Classical Kids believes that singing is primary for all music-making. The series offers more than 40 classical songs written out, and students are encouraged to write their own lyrics to well-known orchestral pieces and sing them.
2. *Performing on instruments, alone and with others, a varied repertoire.* These Teacher's Notes offer more than 50 pieces written out for recorders, glockenspiels, piano or guitar.

3. *Improvising melodies, variations and accompaniments.* The series encourages actively "playing with" musical elements, making answering phrases in ABA form, creating melodies based on chords and scales, and improvising variations or canons.
4. *Composing and arranging music within specified guidelines.* Be it creating "music from Neptune," writing ragtime, superimposing melodies, or composing music over which to read script, we seek to fire a child's musical imagination.
5. *Reading and notating music.* All the written-out pieces can be photocopied for classroom reading. Some titles include step-by-step descriptions for learning to read notation.
6. *Listening to, analyzing and describing music.* Musical terminology, instrumentation and form are explained. We encourage students to graph the "musical spine" of scenes in terms of tempo, instrumentation and mood. Classical Kids is particularly interested in helping students develop a descriptive vocabulary to interpret and listen to music imaginatively.
7. *Evaluating music and music performances.* All the music on the recordings has been expressly recorded to reflect images in the script. This provides an opportunity to talk about the performances and compare them to other recordings of the same piece.
8. *Understanding relationships between music and the other arts as well as disciplines outside the arts.* Classical Kids offers something unique for the last two criteria (8 and 9). The Discussion and Activities sections link music to other arts and subjects.
9. *Understanding music in relation to history and culture.* In the Background section of every scene, the music is set in its historical context. You will find a wealth of anecdotal facts and vivid descriptions of the times, without having to go to a library for outside sources.

(Adapted from National Standards for Arts Education *published by Music Educators National Conference. Copyright 1994. Reproduced with permission. The complete National Standards and additional materials related to the standards are available from Music Educators National Conference, 1806 Robert Fulton Drive, Reston, VA 22091.)*

Synopsis of the Story

After the dramatic take-off of Bach's music into space aboard *Voyager II,* we find ourselves in the living room of eight-year-old Elizabeth. She is practicing the famous Minuet in G when Mr. Bach arrives with his magic orchestra and rollicking boys' choir. In a lively and touching conversation, Elizabeth learns about his life... his 20 children, his stay in prison, Anna Magdalena, the exciting family picnics and concerts... and his music, including a composition based on a well-loved nursery rhyme. Only at the end do we learn the reason for Bach's visit: "So that my music will never again be forgotten... for wherever my music is being played, I am alive."

Things to Talk About Before the Recording

- Ask your students how many brothers and sisters they have. Bach had 20, of whom 14 lived.
- This story travels forward in time. Can your class name other books, movies or television shows that bring a historical figure forward in time?
- Talk about students' favorite music. When do they listen to it? What music does the rest of their family prefer? Make a class list of hits to see if there are gender differences in preferences.
- Generally, how do your students think classical music differs from or resembles today's "popular music"?
- Set the scene by saying, "Today you are going to meet a man who wrote music more than 300 years ago. Do you think people will be listening to today's music three centuries from today?"
- Do any of your students make up songs in their head or on a keyboard? This recording has a lively section on how to compose based on "All Around the Mulberry Bush."
- Speculate on how different life would have been 300 years ago. List conveniences and toys that people would *not* have had then.
- Tell your class that despite having 20 children, Bach wrote so much music that it would take 60 years just to copy out all the music he wrote!
- Would anyone like to have 19 brothers and sisters?
- As you will hear, this recording combines music, voice and sound effects in layers. How many separate tracks does your class think this would take? [Answer: eight, two stereo soundtracks for each layer. They are all balanced and "distanced" for clarity of script, music and sound effects.]

SCENE 1: NASA, BACH AND BOYS ARRIVE

LENGTH OF SCENE: 6:59 TAPE STARTING POINT: SIDE 1/0:00 CD TRACK 1

BEGINS: *"T minus 10-9-8."*

ENDS: *"Soprano."*

The Story

After the countdown, Bach's music is launched into space. We learn what is aboard the *Voyager* spacecraft. Elizabeth is having an argument with her mother about practicing. Bach arrives and helps her play a minuet, accompanied by his choir of boys and magic orchestra.

The Music

- Orchestral Suite No. 3, Mvt 1
- Minuet in G
- Gigue in G (French Suite No. 5)

Background Information

The Voyager Space Probe

The opening countdown and sound effects stir our curiosity. What has Bach's music to do with outer space? The answer is that three of his pieces are now floating somewhere beyond the outer planets: the Brandenburg Concerto No. 2 (Mvt 1), the Prelude and Fugue in C (Book II of the Well-Tempered Clavier) and the Partita No. 3 for Unaccompanied Violin (Gavotte).

Voyager carries about 90 minutes of music and voices on a gold-plated record. The aluminum jacket cover is engraved with pictures describing how to play the recording with the cartridge and stylus provided.

The famous biologist Lewis Thomas was asked by astronomer Carl Sagan what music he would have chosen to represent humankind in space. Thomas's answer: "I would have sent all the works of Johann Sebastian Bach, but that would have been boasting."

Discussion and Activities

Space Talk

Questions to ask:

- How many sounds and pictures can you remember from the *Voyager* list?
- Imagine you are an alien from Neptune meeting *Voyager*. Given the contents described, what would be your impression of the planet Earth?
- What else would you have included on *Voyager* to show what humans are really like? What music?
- As your class listens again to the NASA take-off, supply art materials to create a collage of *Voyager*'s contents. [Examples: whales, children, birds, etc.]
- Prepare an imaginary interview with an alien from Neptune. What do you think might be its impression of earth after spending 24 hours here?

At Home

Questions to ask:

- Elizabeth is having an argument with her mother. Do you ever fight with your parents over practicing an instrument? Have you found ways of solving this problem?
- Bach talks of his "magic orchestra." What might be today's equivalent to a prince's private orchestra? [Answer: synthesizer.]

- If you could choose someone, fictional or real, to visit your house, who would it be? What would you especially want to show your visitor. A treasured possession or pet? What questions would you ask?

A Difficult Name

The nomenclature of Bach's family is confusing. This is partly because many members had the same first name, Johann. Individuals were then identified by the middle name (e.g., Sebastian Bach) or by their initials (e.g., C.P.E. for Carl Philipp Emanuel Bach).

- Elizabeth, like many children, has trouble pronouncing Bach's name. Have the class practice saying "Johann Sebastian Bach" like on the recording.

Exploring the Music

Space Music

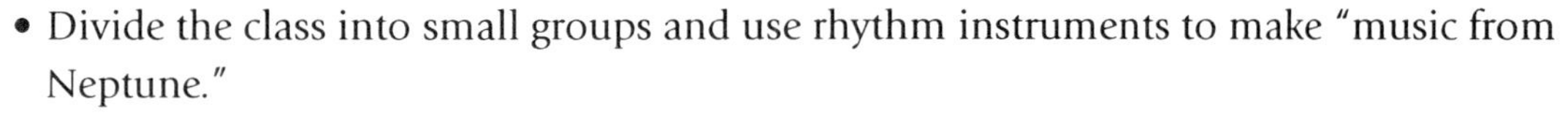

- Divide the class into small groups and use rhythm instruments to make "music from Neptune."

- The opening Orchestral Suite that plays during the NASA countdown is a wonderfully expansive piece. Encourage your class to conduct it or create a dance to express the idea of music spanning the universe.

The Harpsichord and Clavichord

The piano we use today (which is called a pianoforte) was unknown during Bach's lifetime. However, just before he died, he was shown an early version of this instrument, called the fortepiano, by the King of Prussia. He was not impressed.

The three preferred keyboard instruments in Bach's time were the organ, harpsichord and clavichord. The organ is still common today. The harpsichord plucks the strings with quills rather than striking them with hammers. The clavichord is a small personal instrument, similar to the piano in that leather hammers strike the strings to create loud and soft notes. This instrument is seldom heard today because it is quiet, fragile and rare.

Although Bach sometimes featured the harpsichord as a solo instrument, he most frequently used it with a cello in the role of "continuo." You can hear it behind most Baroque orchestral pieces.

Questions to ask and activities to suggest:

- Compare a harpsichord recording of Bach's Gigue (French Suite No. 5) with the piano version on this recording. Which do you prefer? How would you express the difference between the two?

- Look at the picture of a Baroque harpsichord on page 12. How does it appear different from today's grand piano? [Answers: the keys colors are the opposite, harpsichords are highly decorated; harpsichords are more rectangular.]
- Cut a large piece of paper in the shape of a harpsichord lid and decorate it.

Bach's Minuet in G

The minuet that Elizabeth practices is undoubtedly Bach's most famous piece for children. He wrote it in Anna Magdalena's Notebook to teach his wife and children how to play the harpsichord. Here are some suggestions of how to "play with" this timeless piece. Begin by copying out the first phrase on the blackboard, as written here.

Then tell your students to:

1. Number your fingers from 1 to 5, starting with the thumb and ending with the little finger. Put your right hand on the desk and "play" the first phrase using finger numbers: 5-1-2-3-4-5-1-1. If you had a piano, you would now be playing Bach!
2. What would be the second phrase? [Answer: move your hand further right on your "piano" and play: 3-1-2-3-4-5-1-1.] Figure out the rest of the fingering by playing adjacent notes with adjacent fingers.
3. Draw the shape of the first phrase using lines and dashes:
   Continue "drawing" the rest of the piece in this manner.

4. The best way to remember a melody is to sing it. Make up lyrics to Bach's Minuet and sing! For example:

   Come, join me in the meadow green,
   Dance, little children, dance with me, etc.

5. The first half of the Minuet in G is written here in its original form. More advanced players can play it in two parts: the top melody and the bass line both played in the treble register.

Minuet in G Major

Let's Dance

In this scene, we hear two Baroque dances. A minuet is a graceful precursor to the waltz in 3/4 time. A gigue is a faster dance in 6/8 time.

Find a book on 18th-century dress and show your students how ladies wore wide skirts padded out with "panniers" (baskets filled with straw) strapped to the hips under the dresses. How would this influence the dance? [Answers: there was more vertical movement than horizontal; people scarcely touched except with gloved hands.]

Every class can dance this simple minuet. Line up your students in two long rows, so that each child touches fingers with a partner. Now play Bach's minuet and dance as follows:

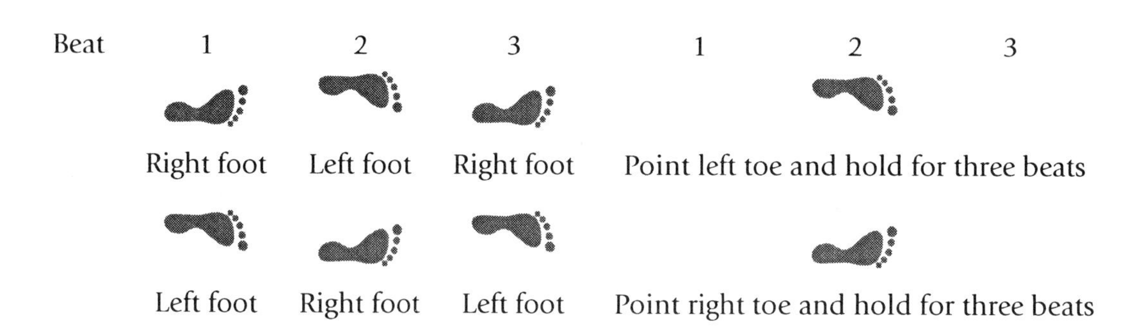

Variations

During the middle section (B) of Bach's minuet, vary the dance with these suggestions:

1. Face each other, step into center as before, with right-left-right and touch palms for the next bar.
2. Step back apart off left foot.
3. Six beats to pass on right, six beats to pass on left.
4. Bow and curtsy at the end.

Scene 2: The Duke, Jail and Organ

LENGTH OF SCENE: 6:35 TAPE STARTING POINT: SIDE 1/6:59 CD TRACKS 2–3

BEGINS: *"Because I worked for the wrong duke."*

ENDS: *"It was like playing music on a skyscraper."*

The Story

Bach talks about his life and problems at the Duke of Weimar's. We also learn about his stay in jail and why he was sent there. The choir boys introduce the instruments of the orchestra. Bach enthusiastically describes his favorite instrument: the organ.

The Music

- "Jesu, Joy of Man's Desiring"
- Chromatic Fantasy
- Prelude in B Minor
- Chorale Prelude: "Allein Gott"

Background Information

Bach in Jail

In Baroque times, musicians were treated as servants or property. The Duke of Weimar was so angry when Bach accepted a job with the Prince of Cöthen that he put him under house arrest for a month. While in jail, Bach composed the famous Prelude in C, which is heard in the next scene.

Germany during Bach's Time

Germany as we know it did not exist in Bach's time. It was composed of about 300 separate principalities, each with its own court and chapel. Princes considered musicians as essential to their lives as their cooks and private army.

In reading about his travels, we should remember that Bach lived his whole life in what was formerly known as East Germany. Unlike Handel, who traveled all his life, Bach never moved more than 100 miles from his birthplace at Eisenach. Ask your students to locate on a map the places mentioned on this recording: Weimar, Cöthen, Leipzig and Brandenburg.

A Famous Competition

During his lifetime, Bach was more famous as an organist than as a composer. Even as a teenager, he was often asked to test various organs around Germany because of his acute ear and profound knowledge of the instrument.

In a famous incident, Bach was invited to compete with Louis Marchand, the famous organist from the dazzling court of Louis XIV. However, the competition never occurred: Marchand heard Bach practicing and hurriedly left town.

Discussion and Activities

- Discuss with your class evidence of how Elizabeth's attitude is changing toward Bach. [Answer: she defends him against the boys and his jailer; she is visibly impressed with his playing the piano and organ; she sympathizes with his loneliness in jail.]

The Music Industry

The status of musicians has changed greatly over the centuries. We clearly do not view musicians as servants now. Instead, we treat them as heroes, almost gods. Ask your students:

- Talk about musical superstars today. Discuss the role of recording and publicity in creating musical superstars.

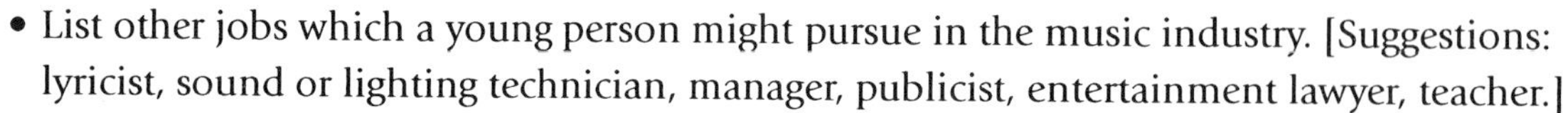

- List other jobs which a young person might pursue in the music industry. [Suggestions: lyricist, sound or lighting technician, manager, publicist, entertainment lawyer, teacher.]
- Bach was known as a great improviser. What kind of music uses this skill today? [Answers: jazz, popular music.]

- What other instruments do you think Bach would play? [Suggestions: piano, synthesizer.] What special feature do these instruments offer? [Answer: varied dynamics.]

Life in a Musical Family

- Is it likely that today Bach would have had as many children?
- How were Bach's children useful to his musical career? [Answers: singing, playing, cutting reeds for the woodwinds, copying out parts.]
- In Bach's time, children often chose the same career as their parents. Do you think you will make that choice? Name some examples of musicians, actors or athletes who have followed in their parents' footsteps.

Exploring the Music

Jesu, Joy of Man's Desiring

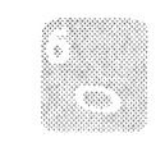

- Play "Jesu, Joy" again for your students. Is the main melody in the strings or the woodwinds? [Answer: woodwinds.] Ask your students to raise their hands when they hear the main theme return after the middle section.

- Any melody is best learned by singing it. Have the class write some new words for "Jesu, Joy" and sing it. For example:

  Day is done, the night is still,
  Moon shines brightly on the hill, etc.

"Jesu, Joy" is one of Bach's most popular melodies. Like Beethoven's "Ode to Joy," it is simple to play because it moves basically step by step and uses only five notes.

- Play "Jesu, Joy" as it is written here in simplified piano form. It can also be played on two recorders from this score: One recorder takes the top melody line, and the other plays the accompanying line immediately below it in the treble clef.
- Add glockenspiels: Play the melody, the first note of each bar or even a series of repeated D's.

- Ask your students to describe the images, ideas or feelings that come to mind as they listen to "Jesu, Joy." Have them draw or practice a movement exercise to bring out its evocative quality.

Jesu, Joy of Man's Desiring

2 recorders on treble line

Arr. Susan Hammond

The King of Instruments

The organ is a fascinating — and huge — instrument. It can have as many as 3,600 pipes! These pipes are organized into sets called stops, which imitate the sound of other instruments (e.g., the flute stop). Each stop has a large wooden handle that is "pulled" to let air flow through into a set of pipes. In Bach's time, young boys were hired to "pump the bellows" that created this air pressure. These look much like the fireplace bellows you use to fan a fire at home. In this recording, the "bird" sound is made by forcing air through two tiny organ pipes partially submerged in a container of water.

- To appreciate what a "full organ" sounds like, listen to Bach's exciting Toccata in D Minor, available at any library or store. Bach is quoted as saying, "Above all, I must know whether an organ has good lungs!"
- Notice that although the "bell" doesn't actually play "in time" with the piece, your ears gradually perceive it that way.
- Bach called the organ the "king of instruments." What would you consider the most powerful instrument today? [Suggestions: synthesizer, electric guitar, drum sets.]

The Organ

Most organs have two to four keyboards (called manuals) and a pedal-board, which looks like a large keyboard played by the feet.

- Plan a class visit to a local church that has a pipe organ. Ask the organist to play a piece by Bach. Can he or she demonstrate the keyboards, pipes and stops for you? Notice how you can play three melodies on three different keyboards, each with a different sound.

- In art class, build an organ out of craft materials. Use paper rolls for pipes, and decorate them in the Baroque style. Three flat boxes can be painted black and white to look like keyboards. The illustration here can serve as a model. Alternatively, photocopy and color it for younger classes.

Tuning and Technique: Bach's Two Great Innovations

The *pitch* of a note most often depends on the length of the vibrating string or pipe. Large organs can have pipes up to 64 feet in length (the equivalent of a three-story building). The lowest notes are more "felt" through the feet than actually "heard." Try these simple class exercises to demonstrate the science of tuning.

- Discover whether a longer string makes a higher or lower note by stretching an elastic band and "pinging" it. Then shorten it with a knot and "ping" it again. Try to keep the tension the same as this can affect pitch, too. Which length produces a higher note? [Answer: The shorter loops are higher in pitch.]
- Look inside a piano to see how the bass strings are longer on the metal harp.
- Can there be another factor affecting pitch? [Answer: Yes, the tension on a string.]
- Can someone bring in a violin and demonstrate this?

- Research the fundamental change that Bach made to the tuning system, called "equal temperament." By dividing the octave into 12 equal semitones, he made it possible to play in all 24 keys (12 major and 12 minor). This is how a piano is tuned today and has become the foundation for all western music.

Few people know that Bach also changed *technique,* the way we use our fingers on the keyboard. Previously, musicians had played with only the middle three fingers and in a flattened position. Bach insisted that the thumb and all the fingers be used in a curved position. This innovation was as important as his new tuning system in making possible the virtuostic music of later eras. Ask your class:

- Can someone demonstrate the proper hand position for piano playing?
- "Play a scale" on your desk. First play the eight notes of a scale using only your middle three fingers and crossing your second finger over your fourth. Then, play the same eight notes using your thumb and crossing it under your middle finger. See how curving the fingers creates a space for the thumb to make a smooth transition between the third and fourth note of the scale.

The Prelude in B Minor

As you can hear, the Prelude in B Minor is a serene meditation. Ask you students:

- What do you know about the effect of relaxation in sport, dance, music? While listening to a restful piece by Bach, try a relaxation exercise with the class (close your eyes, tense and release muscles, describe a relaxing scene).
- How does the mood of the Prelude in B Minor match the words about Bach in jail? [Answer: The Prelude is slow and in a minor key, while Bach talks about missing his family.]

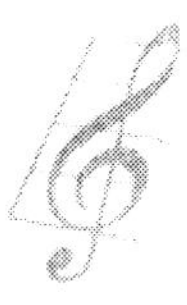

Scene 3: Prince, Walks and Practicing

LENGTH OF SCENE: 10:02 TAPE STARTING POINT: SIDE 1/13:34 CD TRACKS 4–6

BEGINS: *"Imagine putting a man like you in jail."*

ENDS: *"Ja, I am Mr. Bach."*

The Story

Bach describes family life in a castle, the Brandenburg Concerti and choirboy pranks. He talks about his famous walk to hear Buxtehude. Bach tells how he taught his own children how to compose and about his first wife's death when he was away at the spa of Carlsbad. He shows Elizabeth how to make a piece from chords and then explains attitudes toward girls during Baroque times.

The Music

- Brandenburg Concerto No. 5, Mvt 3
- Flute Sonata in C, Mvt 2
- Organ: "Es ist das Heil"
- Orchestral Suite No. 2, Mvt 6
- Violin Sonata in E, Mvt 2
- Prelude in C (Book I of Well-Tempered Clavier)
- Orchestral Suite No. 2, Mvt 2

Background Information

Traveling Bach

Bach and Beethoven traveled far less than Handel, Mozart and Tchaikovsky. Nonetheless, the story of Bach's teenage walk of 260 miles (420 kilometers) to hear Buxtehude play demonstrates his fierce desire to learn more about the organ. On that trip, Bach was rummaging for food in a garbage heap outside an inn when he found two fish heads containing some ducats in them. It is believed that a secret admirer had hidden some money to help the young composer on his journey.

Bach also made two unsuccessful journeys to visit Handel (see the Classical Kids recording *Hallelujah Handel!*). The two composers were born in the same year of 1685, only 20 miles (32 kilometers) apart, but never met.

Bach also traveled with Prince Leopold to the Carlsbad spa. Any visiting prince would bring along his friends, servants and musicians to help pass the hours while "taking the waters." These spa cures were considered essential in a time when medicines were less developed than they are now. Many European spas, specializing in either water or mud treatments, are still in operation today.

The Bach Family

Bach's first wife was his cousin, Maria Barbara. He once caused a scandal by inviting her to sing in church. At that time, women were excluded from performing in church as young boy sopranos sung the top line. Maria Barbara gave birth to seven of Bach's 20 children.

Typical of a time when boys took their father's occupation, all of Bach's sons were taught composing, but only three became composers. This is why we have "generations of Bachs making music." Ironically, Bach's three composing sons, W.F. Bach, C.P.E. and J.C. all considered their father's music old-fashioned and became pioneers in the new Classical style.

Discussion and Activities

Court Life

The castle was the center of German life in the 1700s. One of the most musical courts was at Cöthen where Bach spent six of his happiest years as Kapellmeister (music master) to Prince Leopold. There he composed almost all the instrumental music we enjoy on concert programs today: chamber works, concerti and solo harpsichord or piano pieces.

Physically, the castle at Cöthen was unique. A large moat surrounded what had been the medieval jousting field. Bach would wake each morning to the sound of birds and children, then fall asleep to the slow turning of the water wheel.

Ask your students to:

- Make a map or picture of this castle as you see it in your mind's eye. Include the castle, stables, chapel, separate kitchen in case of a fire, horse yards, moat, water wheel and draw bridge.
- Pretend you are one of Bach's children and plan a day at Cöthen. What games would you play in a castle? What jobs could you do? Has anyone in class visited a real castle?
- Look at a picture of a castle bedroom with four-poster bed. Talk about all the objects found there (chamber pots, wig stands, clocks, etc.). Why do you think the beds are so high? [Answer: to get further away from the cold floor, mice and rats.] Why do the beds have curtains? [Answer: for warmth.] How do people climb into them at night? [Answer: a ladder.]

- Research daily life at the Sun King's castle in France (Louis XIV). There are wonderful details about how the whole court had to rigidly follow the schedule of the king: get up when he rose, go to bed when he retired, pray when he was in chapel, start eating only after him, nap when he napped.

Traveling Musicians

Talk about the differences between touring musicians 300 years ago and today. As a teen, Bach travelled simply on foot. Later, he traveled by horse-drawn coach, with a harpsichord, violin, music scores, court clothes and wigs, all strapped onto the roof.

Ask your class:

- Has anyone in your class seen musicians setting up for a concert? How do they travel? What do they bring into a concert venue? [Answer: lighting systems, sound systems, sets, costumes, merchandising items, teams of publicists and technicians.]
- What star or famous person would you like to meet? Write that person a letter introducing yourself and asking questions you might be uncomfortable asking in person.

- As an exercise in local geography, and to understand the scope of Bach's walk, create a map of concentric circles from your home: a block; a mile or kilometer; 10 miles or kilometers; 60, 150, 260 miles or kilometers. Establish landmarks at each distance.
  - Can you figure out how long it would take to travel 260 miles or 420 kilometers by horseback (20 miles/day or 30 kilometers/day), car (60 miles/hour or 100 kilometers/hour), plane (500 miles/hour or 800 kilometers/hour) or spacecraft (17,000 miles/hour or 27,0000 kilometers/hour).
  - Plan a three-week walking adventure from your home: how would you arrange food, finding your way, keeping in communication, raising spirits, managing money, making sleeping arrangements?
- Bach tells us about an emergency in his family when he was traveling: the death of his first wife. Have you ever had an emergency in your family? How was it solved?

Practicing

By today's standards, Bach's teaching methods would seem very severe: his students were not allowed to touch the keyboard before the age of nine. Even then, they were not allowed to play a piece until they had completed a full six months of exercises. Ask those children who play an instrument:

- At what age did you begin taking lessons? Are you studying more than one instrument?
- What did you learn in the beginning lessons? Demonstrate on a piano, violin or other instrument.
- Talk about the differences between practicing a piece (or game) and playing it.
- How do students perceive the difference between work and play? Can one include the other?
- Compile a list of favorite games. Do any of those games require practicing, or is merely playing them actually practicing?

Role Playing with Contemporary Issues

- Bach apologizes for boasting about his music at Cöthen. Try some role playing on bragging. Is it possible to be proud of one's work without being conceited? What is the difference in expression?
- Elizabeth objects to what we would call "gender stereotyping" in Bach's comments about his girls. Certainly, in earlier times, roles were more specifically defined. What were boys of the same age expected to do 300 years ago, as opposed to girls?
- Are there any differences today in gender expectations?
- Suggest students pretend they are part of Bach's large family and role-play a scenario between Bach and one of his daughters or sons. [Suggestions: a daughter wants to sing publicly, a son does not want to be a musician.]

Exploring the Music

Bach's Brandenburg Concerti

If you listen carefully, you can hear how Baroque orchestral works alternate two levels of sound: a small group of soloists (called the concertino) and a larger group of accompanying string players (called the ripieno).

The famous Brandenburg Concerti were written for a duke who lived near Cöthen. They are wonderfully buoyant works, well worth bringing into class. Here are some highlights.

- The Second Brandenburg Concerto features two trumpets. It was included on the *Voyager* space probe (Track 1).
- The Fourth Brandenburg Concerto eloquently interweaves two flutes.
- The Fifth Brandenburg, which is heard in this scene, is the most popular of the set.
  - How does this second movement suit the animated antics of castle life described here? [Answer: a lively rhythm.]
  - What instruments are in the concertino? [Answer: flute and solo violin.]

Bach's Orchestral Suites

It is easy to confuse Bach's four Orchestral Suites with his six Brandenburg Concerti. In order of appearance, here are the movements from the Orchestral Suites as they are heard on this recording.

- Orchestral Suite No. 3, Mvt 1: Opening NASA take-off (Track 1).
  - Why do students think this music was chosen? [Answer: trumpets pealing across the sky.]
- Orchestral Suite No. 2, Mvt 6: Bach talks about life with the Prince (Track 5).
  - How does this music reflect life at court? [Answer: its rhythm is stately, royal.] Walk to it in an elegant way, remembering the cumbersome court clothes.
- Orchestral Suite No. 2, Mvt 2: Bach talks about the position of girls in Baroque times (Track 6).
  - How does the music mirror the formalism of the time? [Answer: again, it is a stately dance.]
- Orchestral Suite No. 2, Mvt 4, The Flute Badinerie: Bach talks about "the concerts we made!" (Track 8).
  - This favorite piece captures a busy scene. How? [Answer: The music is fast, exciting, twirling.]
- Orchestral Suite No. 3, Mvt 3, Air on the G String: Bach talks about the Midnight Manuscript (Track 9).
  - Describe the relationship between words and music here. [Answer: the glowing screens reflect the sorrow of losing his parents, then the moonlit scene in the attic.]

The Famous First Prelude in C

This section on chords talks about one of Bach's most well-loved melodies: the opening Prelude from Book I of the Well-Tempered Clavier. Bach originally wrote it in Wilhelm Friedemann's Notebook to teach his oldest son how to play the harpsichord. He later copied it into Anna Magdalena's Notebook.

Bach's Minuet in G and Beethoven's "Ode to Joy" are both built on adjacent notes of a scale. In contrast, Bach's Prelude in C and Beethoven's "Shepherd's Theme" are built on the notes of a chord.

• If you have a piano, play the chord C-E-G, C-E-G reading upwards.

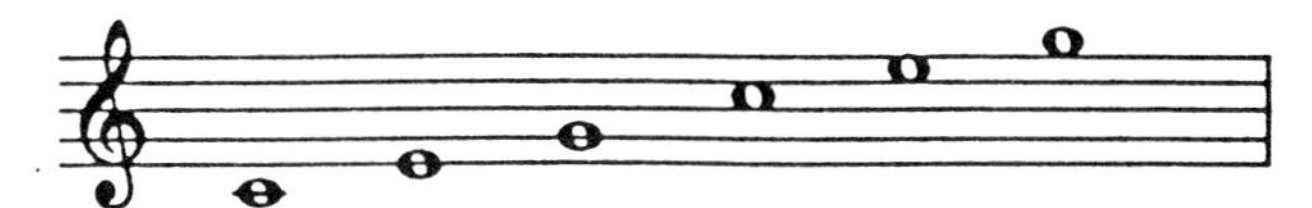

Bach arranged the notes for this prelude in this manner:

• Have your students rearrange the notes to make their own melody.
• Here are some other melodies built on a chord to explore with your class.

I've Got Sixpence

Taps

Beethoven's Sixth Symphony

Mozart's Eine kleine Nachtmusik

Scene 4: Anna Magdalena, Concerts, Children, Young Life

LENGTH OF SCENE: 8:30 TAPE STARTING POINT: SIDE 2/0:00 CD TRACKS 7–9

BEGINS: *"Who's she?"*

ENDS: *"The name Bach came to mean musician."*

The Story

Bach tells about his life with Anna Magdalena. He describes their family concerts and talks about his 20 children. We hear the story of the Midnight Manuscript.

The Music

- "Bist du bei mir"
- Orchestral Suite No. 2, Flute Badinerie
- Orchestral Suite No. 3, Air for the G String

Background Information

Bach's Family

Anna Magdalena was only 20 when she met the 40-year-old Bach. She had a beautiful soprano voice and was the daughter of a trumpeter from a neighboring town. In addition to having 13 children, Anna Magdalena worked hard as Bach's copyist. Eventually her handwriting became indistinguishable from his own.

Bach really did have 20 children. Of them, ten died, five lived to middle age and five to old age. Most of the long-lived children were composers. Here's a frivolous thought: is composing good for your health?

In addition to his 20 children, Bach had 17 grandchildren, 14 great-grandchildren and one great-great-grandchild. The line ends with Carolina Wilhelmina Bach's death in 1871.

With all those children, it is tragic that Anna Magdalena died alone in a poorhouse in 1765, 15 years after Bach's death.

An interesting footnote: although Beethoven was not particularly impressed with Bach's music, he staged a benefit concert for Bach's last surviving daughter, Regine Susanna.

Bach's Lost Childhood

Unfortunately, both of Bach's parents died within a year of each other. He was raised from the age of 10 by his brother, Johann Christoph, who was 14 years older than he.

Discussion and Activities

Wigs

Talk about wigs with your class. Children who hate to comb their hair will enjoy these questions and answers!

- Do people have their own hair underneath? [Answer: Yes.]
- Do people take off their wigs at night? [Answer: Yes, they mount them on wig stands.]

- How much do wigs weigh? [Answer: 2 to 5 pounds/ 4.5 to 11 kilograms.]
- How do they keep their shape? [Answer: rags to fill in the hair, pins to keep it in place.]
- Was the hair all human? [Answer: some of it came from horse tails.]
- Why are wigs white? [Answer: flour or lead compound was blown onto the hair by servants in the "powder room" — a name we still use today.]
- How did the powder stick to the wig? [Answer: using pig's fat. Imagine the smell of rancid fat, and you can see why perfume was invented in France!]
- How did people move with high wigs balanced on their heads? [Answer: Inside the wig was lever they could use to lower the hair.]
- What is the purpose of wigs? [Answer: to give stature and elegance to the wearer.]
- What about lice? [Answer: Lice were indeed prevalent. It is often said that the 18th century was the "century of scratching." At elegant dinners, each place setting would include a silver claw for scratching at the lice that thrived on the flour and pig's fat in the wigs.]

After the Baroque era, wigs became shorter. We see this in Mozart's small pony-tail and Beethoven's wild natural hair. Wigs fell out of fashion by the end of the 1700s.

The Midnight Manuscript

Bach describes how his older brother took away a piece of music.

- Ask your students why they think he might have done this. [Answers: they were valuable originals; Johann Christoph thought the music was too difficult.]
- Has anyone in class had the experience of someone taking away something very precious? How did they feel? What did they do?
- While listening to the Air for the G String (Orchestral Suite No. 3, Mvt 3), draw the haunting scene of Bach stealing into the attic to look at some music by moonlight. Alternatively, let this serene music suggest its own images.

Remembering the Past: Guest Books and Family Trees

Guest Books

Musicians who visited the Bach household were asked to leave a short song in the guest book. This unique guest book reflected perfectly the focus of the Bach family.

- Suggest that students design a guest book for their own homes to reflect their interests. Over the years, they will be surprised by how many people they would have forgotten without such a record. Have students:
  - Design the covers and inside format of their guest book in art class.
  - Design an inside page that includes the date and their age.
  - Set a theme or style. Would they prefer that people write jokes? Cartoons? Funny poems?
  - Punch holes and use colored wool or gimp to bind the guest book.

Family Trees

Many people are now interested in genealogy. Tell your students to:

- Research Bach's family tree: Question parents and other relatives about their past.
- Design and decorate a family tree to hang somewhere special at home.

Home Concerts

Before television and radio, home concerts were a popular form of entertainment. Suggest your students put on a house concert with their friends for parents and neighbors.

- Plan your musical program with as much variety as possible.
- What other preparations are necessary? [Suggestions: arranging music, seating, tickets, serving refreshments.]
- Record the concert and give it as a present to someone special.

Exploring the Music

Three Contrasting Pieces

This scene juxtaposes three of Bach's most wonderful pieces: "Bist du bei mir," the Flute Badinerie and the Air for the G String.

Many people have said that "Bist du bei mir" is their favorite piece on this recording. All ages seem to respond to its quiet beauty. Experts differ on whether he actually composed it or whether it was written by G.H. Stoelzel. The question is not very important as Bach obviously admired it enough to give it as a wedding present to his beloved second wife.

Bist du bei mir

- Have students play "Bist du bei mir," arranged for two recorders on page 29. The most familiar sections are found in the bars ending with the "Fine."

- Suggest that students write their own lyrics to it.

Flute Badinerie

- Enjoy dancing or clapping to infectious beat of the Flute Badinerie. While we were recording, we came to nickname it the "Bach Rock."
- How does the music suit the image of "And the concerts we made!"? [Answer: fast, exciting, with a strong beat.]

Air for the G String

- The Air for the G String, which plays under the text of the Midnight Manuscript, is one of Bach's loveliest melodies. Listen particularly to how the bass steps slowly downward while the melody arches upward. Also listen to how the harpsichordist improvises that part. Bach provides only the chord structure and the bass line. The harpsichordist must spontaneously fill in the other notes, drawing melodies in the other parts.

Choral Reading

In some ways, describing this next activity is harder than actually doing it. Be assured that it is well worth the trouble! Several teachers have requested that the entire script to *Mr. Bach Comes to Call* be published so their students can read it aloud over music. They are right... it can be an extremely moving experience! Even the most simple sentences can become more poignant, exciting and even profound when read with music behind them.

- Read aloud from the following page the words to two contrasting sections from this scene. Remind your students to take their time to space the words out over the phrases.

Selection No. 1: Flute Badinerie from the Orchestral Suite No. 2
"And the concerts we made! All the excitement... the children running around... getting the candles ready... putting the music pages on the music stands... that was a job! Poor Anna Magdalena was always copying out some last-minute music... shouting at the children to get dressed... shoes, choir gowns, rosin for the bows, reeds for the woodwinds, wigs... you know, we had to wear wigs... Itch. Stank. Hot. Powder all over your clothes. They were a great, big nuisance, those stupid wigs... and always getting lost... But I miss the concerts!"

Selection No. 2: Air for the G String, Orchestral Suite No. 3
"My brother Christoph used to lock his music up in the cupboard because he thought I was not ready for it. Of course I was ready! So, in the middle of the night, when everyone was sound asleep, I sneaked out of my bed, stuck my hand through the slats of the cupboard door and pulled out the music. There I was, sitting at the table, the moon shining through the window... I was not allowed a candle... copying the music out, page by page, note by note... And then my brother found out."

Have students select another passage from a book or their journals and read it over one of these pieces of music. See how reading aloud over music can change your appreciation and interpretation of the written word!

Bist du bei mir

2 recorders

Arr. Susan Hammond

Scene 5: Picnics, An Adventure in Music

LENGTH OF SCENE: 5:32   TAPE STARTING POINT: SIDE 2/8:30   CD TRACKS 10–11

BEGINS: *"Oh boy, food..."*

ENDS: *Bach sighs.*

The Story

Bach tells about his large family picnics. He teaches Elizabeth about composing.

The Music

- Orchestral Suite No. 3, Gigue
- Adventure in Music on "Pop Goes the Weasel"

Background Information

Bach's roots have been traced back over 200 years to Viet Bach, a baker and zither player who died about 1576. Between then and 1850, 60 Bachs held important musical posts in Germany.

Unlike many biographies, *Mr. Bach Comes to Call* portrays the composer as sociable, confident and playful. Here is some evidence for this characterization:

- Almost every musician who visited Leipzig dropped in on the Bach household for an extended period.
- Students sometimes lived with the family for as long as two years.
- Bach loved to drink the newly imported drink, coffee, at Zimmermann's Café. He even wrote the Coffee Cantata singing its praises.
- A more personal side of Bach is found in his song-poem "Reflections of a Tobacco Smoker" and the tender love letter to Anna Magdalena.

Discussion and Activities

Music as a Social Activity

Singing is wonderful at family, religious or school occasions. Bach describes huge family picnics of 150 people. Imagine getting together with enough relatives to fill five average-sized classrooms!

- Ask your students about their favorite family occasions. When and where do they take place? What do the grownups do? What do the children do? Does anyone help with preparations?
- Suggest that your students print up a song-sheet for your next school picnic.
- Compile a list of multi-generational or camp songs and sing them (e.g., "I've Got Six-pence," "She'll be Comin' Round the Mountain").
- In art class, have students make a mural of their impressions of a Bach family picnic. Research children's games of the time. Include scattered groups of musicians in the portrayal.
- Encourage younger classes to gallop to the orchestral gigue.

Exploring the Music

The Adventure in Music

This is definitely one of the most popular parts of *Mr. Bach Comes to Call.* Although Bach obviously did not write this nursery-rhyme fugue, it is a fine way to demonstrate the craft of Baroque composition. In it, we experiment with two Baroque techniques: playing tunes upside down and superimposing several melodies on top of each other. Explore this Adventure in Music as follows:

- Sing "Pop Goes the Weasel," then learn it upside-down as recorded here. Divide the class into two groups and put the two versions on top of each other.
- "In Dulce Jubilo" can be found in many hymn or Christmas books. Sing it on top of your "Pop Goes the Weasel." Try singing it as a round.
- Continue to play with inverting tunes on the principle that "what goes up must come down." Sing "Twinkle, Twinkle Little Star" upside down as shown below (Voice 1 is in black circles, Voice 2 in clear circles). Try putting the two versions on top of each other.
- Play with superimposition by seeing if other songs will fit on top of each other (e.g., "Hot Cross Buns," "Frère Jacques" and "Mary Had a Little Lamb").

Scene 6: Goldberg, The Art of Fugue and Goodbye

LENGTH OF SCENE: 8:36 TAPE STARTING POINT: SIDE 2/14:02 CD TRACKS 12–14

BEGINS: *"At home, you know, we had wonderful concerts."*

ENDS: *"Here is something from one of my cantatas."*

The Story

We hear the story of the Goldberg Variations. As Bach describes the Art of Fugue, we learn more about composing. He shares some of his regrets, hopes and beliefs with Elizabeth. At the end of the recording, his "boys" sing a bouncing movement from a cantata.

The Music

- Goldberg Variations
- The Art of Fugue
- "Leibster Jesu"
- Flute Sonata in C (Mvt 4)
- "We Hasten" (Cantata 78)

Background Information

"Old Bach is Here"

Late in life, Bach went to visit his new grandchild at the Court of Prussia in Potsdam. His son C.P.E. Bach was Kapellmeister there. To his great delight, the king put aside his flute and gave a warm welcome as he announced, "Gentlemen, Old Bach is here." During his tour of the palace, Bach saw his first fortepiano.

Later, Bach asked the king to give him a tune on which he could improvise. Astounding the entire court with his playing, Bach later sent a rendition of this "Musical Offering" to the king. This piece became the basis for the Art of Fugue heard here.

Failed Eye Operations

Bach died of complications from a second eye operation. It is almost impossible for us to imagine the pain of a needle inserted right into the eye, without anesthetic. Bach had two such operations to treat cataracts. Incidental, the same English doctor also operated unsuccessfully on Handel — thus one surgeon effectively blinded two of our greatest Baroque composers.

Working Hard

Of his life Bach said simply, "I worked hard." He certainly did. At Leipzig, where he spent his last quarter century, Bach had to compose music for four churches. He also taught at St. Thomas School where he taught music and Latin, as well as fulfilling his duties as proctor. Imagine waking up 200 boys at 5:00 a.m. for prayers and making sure they were in bed by 8:00 p.m.!

Despite this, Bach composed an enormous amount of music. It is estimated that it would take a modern-day copyist more than 60 years of full-time copying just to write it out. Although he was helped by his students, children and Anna Magdalena, Bach's life's work represents a pinnacle in music, both in quantity and quality.

Bach's Beliefs and Posterity

This last section reveals some of Bach's fundamental beliefs, regrets and hopes. Here are some quotations from the recording, along with some questions to ask:

- "All my music I wrote for God." For whom is the music of today written? How long will it last?
- "I visit children... because every time my music is being played, I am there, too." Can you see how this might be true?
- "The more you practice, the more you listen... understand... know... appreciate... love." Think about this sequence. What do you think it means?
- "My music was forgotten for 100 years." Fortunately 20-year-old Mendelssohn rescued Bach's music from total neglect 150 years later in London. Modest Bach could never have known how many composers would come to revere him.
- Mozart, who at the age of eight played the organ with Bach's youngest son, Johann Christian: "He is the father of us all, and we are his children."
- Beethoven: "Not brook but sea should be his name." (The German word for brook is *Bach.*)
- Tchaikovsky (who was somewhat less impressed): "I like to play Bach because it is interesting to play a good fugue, but I do not regard him as a great genius."

Discussion and Activities

Boys in the Choir

- Talk about voice changes in boys. At what age does it happen? What is the physiology? Do any boys in your class sing in a choir? How high can they sing? Higher than the girls? Hold a "sing-off" for fun!
- Listen to the last track and find adjectives for the unique sound of a boy's choir. [Suggestions: pure, light, bouncing.]
- Interview one of the boys in Bach's choir. Here are some details to help them get started:
  - Bach's choir boys had to endure long hours practicing in a cold choir loft;
  - Sunday services went from 7:00 a.m. to noon with no breaks for food;
  - The bars had to write out the sermon to prove they had been listening;
  - They performed mandatory torchlit caroling in the streets for the city councilors.

Exploring the Music

Johann Goldberg was a harpsichord player who discovered that Bach's music actually helped put his employer to sleep. Ask your students:

- What music do you like to listen to when you are going to sleep?
- Have your preferences changed as you've grown older?

Elizabeth asks about Bach's "favorite favorites." Here are a few other favorites:

- Favorite instrument: the organ.
- Favorite stringed instrument: the viola, also preferred by Mozart, Beethoven, Schubert.
- Favorite piece of music: St. Matthew Passion. This masterpiece is over four hours long. It asks for two adult choirs, a boys choir, several soloists and a full orchestra. Near the end of his life, Bach laboriously copied out this piece in colored ink.
- List some of your favorite songs, toys, games and places to visit.

On Fugues

- Weave paper placemats with your class to explain a Baroque fugue graphically. Explain that the vertical cuts represent the chords that hold the piece together. The horizontal strips represent the melodies of "subjects" woven into those chords.
- Research the structure of fugues with your older students. Notice how the first "subject" (melody) finishes, then continues as a "counter-subject" to the second entry of the subject in another voice. Fugues are typically written for three to five "voices" and can be performed by solo instruments, choirs or orchestras.

Your Name in Music

Bach was fascinated with the idea of "spelling" in music. For example in the Art of Fugue, we hear his name written out in notes (B-A-C-H).

- Ask students to try to figure out how their names would sound in music. First copy this note-letter chart. The A-to-G scale is repeated as often as necessary to give every letter in the alphabet an equivalent musical note.

Note	Your Letters			
A	A	H	O	V
B	B	I	P	W
C	C	J	Q	X
D	D	K	R	Y
E	E	L	S	Z
F	F	M	T	
G	G	N	U	

- Now, "play" your name, using the letter-notes in various octave positions on the piano.

Numerology in Music

In some ways, M&M can stand for music and math. These often go together, perhaps because music sets up the neurological pathways along which math later follows. All his life, Bach was interested in constructing melodies that "added up" to certain numbers.

The numerology of German letters is as follows:

A = 1	I/J = 9	R = 17
B = 2	K = 10	S = 18
C = 3	L = 11	T = 19
D = 4	M = 12	U/V = 20
E = 5	N = 13	W = 21
F = 6	O = 14	X = 22
G = 7	P = 15	Y = 23
H = 8	Q = 16	Z = 24

For example, Bach's own name added up to 14 (B2 + A1 + C3 + H8). With his initials it adds up to its inverse, 41 (J9 + S18 + BACH14). Poignantly, his last chorale had 14 notes in the tune, and 41 bars in all.

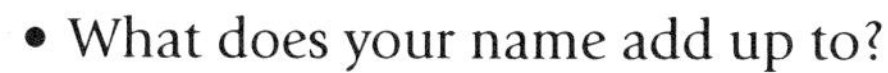

- What does your name add up to?

After the Recording

Questions to ask:

- Do Elizabeth, Bach or the boys change as a result of their adventures together? Have you had experiences that have changed you significantly?
- What parts of the tape did you especially like or dislike? Was the overall production different from what you expected?

Activities:

- Make a storyboard of Bach's life using pictures or words to depict the scenes you remember best.
- Suggest that the class prepare a Bach week. Study the food, customs and costumes of the time. Design some Bach buttons and sing or perform his music on recorders.
- Be a reporter for your school newspaper and interview Bach, Elizabeth and the boys. How is their life the same as, or different from, yours?
- Make a musical scrapbook of your class's favorite music. Poll each other to choose your "Top Ten Tunes." Include some classical music you have heard here.
- Plan a class visit to hear some of Bach's music at a local concert. Invite a local musician to play for you and talk about how playing Bach differs from playing other composers' music. Write and ask your local radio station to play a favorite Bach piece.

Classical Kids and the Integrated Curriculum

This chart and the following 10-day Lesson Plan illustrate the themes and skills developed in these Teacher's Notes for *Mr. Bach Comes to Call.* The page numbers of each activity are noted in the 10-day chart.

There is also a sample question sheet after the Lesson Plan for those teachers wishing to assess their students' skills and knowledge with a short test.

Core Area	Bach
Time Frame	1685–1750
Geography	Germany
Social Studies	• Court life • Position of musicians • Bach in jail • Wigs and dress
Creative Writing	• Retelling the story • Interviews • Time travel • Choral reading
Modern Issues	• Arguments • Gender issues • Family career lines • Bach's beliefs
Other Arts	• Family trees • Guest book • Scene drawing • Sound effects • Dancing minuets
Music	• Space music • Playing and singing • Analyzing of excerpts • Composing on scales and chords • Superimposing tones • Weaving fugues • Biography
Math and Science	• Bach's numerology • Your name in music • Transportation

Suggested Lesson Plan

Week One

MONDAY	TUESDAY	WEDNESDAY	THURSDAY	FRIDAY
Side One • *Voyager*(8) • Time travel • Bach's name (9) • Arguments (9) • Space music (9)	Side Two • Biography (24, 30, 32) • Childhood (26) • Teen walk (19) • Jail (13) • Children (24) • Family picnic (30)	**Social Studies** • Wig research (25, 26) • Court life (20) **Other Arts** • Guest book (26) • Family tree (19, 26) • German (13) • Traveling (20)	**Instruments** • Organ (16, 17) • Harpsichord, clavichord (9, 12) • Tuning (17) • Fingering (17) • Harpsichord decoration (10)	**Minuet in G** • Court dances (10–11) • Melody shape (10–11) • Singing, performing (10–11) • Dancing minuets (10–11) • Practicing (12)

Week Two

MONDAY	TUESDAY	WEDNESDAY	THURSDAY	FRIDAY
Air for G String • Writing to music (27) • Drawing to music (26) • Choral reading (27–28) **Analysis** • Prelude in B Minor (18) • Brandenburg Concerti (22) • Orchestral Suites (22)	**Jesu, Joy** • For two recorders (14–15) • Writing lyrics (14–15) • Analyzing instruments, structure (14) • Choral reading (27)	**Bist du bei mir** • For two recorders (27–29) • Writing lyrics, singing (27) • Bach's beliefs (32–33) **Modern issues** • Bragging, gender stereotypes (21)	**Composition** • Prelude in C (22) • Adventure in Music (31) • Composing music (23) • Music industry (14) • Boy choir (33)	**Fugue Weaving** • Numerology (34) • Your name in music (23) • After the recording (35) • Worksheet (38)

Worksheet for Mr. Bach Comes to Call

1. Bach's year of birth is ________________
2. He died in __________ at the age of _____
3. He lived in the country of ______________
4. His two wives were named ______________ and ________________
5. He had _____children, of whom were composers.
6. Describe Bach's character as you understand if from this recording. ________________
7. Who is Elizabeth? ________________
8. Who are the boys? ________________
9. Tell the story of *Mr. Bach Comes to Call* in your own words. ________________
10. List three sad scenes. ________________
11. List two things that made you laugh. ________________
12. How does Elizabeth's attitude to Bach and his boys change during this story? ________________
13. Describe Bach's childhood. ________________
14. What famous composer was born in the same year as Bach? ________________
15. How many pipes can an organ have? _____
16. What are the three keyboard instruments of the Baroque era? ________________
17. What two other keyboard instruments do we have today? ________________
18. What nursery rhyme does the Adventure in Music use? ________________
19. What is your favorite scene(s)? ________________
20. What is your favorite piece of music? _____

ANSWERS: Cut off this portion before photocopying worksheet. (1) 1685; (2) 1750, 65; (3) Germany; (4) Maria Barabara, Anna Magdalena; (5) 20, 3; (6) playful, competent, talkative, proud; (7) a girl from today; (8) Bach's choir, who come forward in time; (9) N/A; (10) in jail, wife dies, parents die; (11) N/A; (12) she comes to like him; (13) lost parents at 10, lived with brother, went to music school; (14) Handel; (15) 3,600; (16) organ, harpsichord, clavichord; (17) piano, synthesizer; (18) "All Around the Mulberry Bush; (19) N/A; (20) N/A

Classical Kids Awards and Honors

Beethoven Lives Upstairs

AUDIO: Juno Award Best Children's Recording (Canada), Parents' Choice Silver Honor (U.S.), American Library Association Notable Children's Recording Award, Practical Home Schooling Reader Award Music Curriculum Category and Educational Audio Cassette Category (U.S.), Film Advisory Board Award of Excellence (U.S.), Parents' Choice Classic Award (U.S.), Certified Gold Record (Canada), Certified Platinum Record (Canada)

BOOK: Governor General's Award Finalist – Illustration (Canada), Canadian Children's Book Centre Our Choice Recommendation

VIDEO: Emmy Award for Best Children's Program, Parents' Choice Movie Hall of Fame Classic and Gold Awards (U.S.), Dove Foundation Dove Family Approved Seal, Oppenheim Toy Portfolio Platinum Award (U.S.), Film Advisory Board Award of Excellence (U.S.), Gold Camera Award Best Children's Program and Best Direction (U.S.), Certified Multi-Platinum Video (Canada)

CD-ROM: National Parenting Publications Honors Award (U.S.), Film Advisory Board Award of Excellence (U.S.), Curriculum Administrator Top 100 Districts' Choice Award (U.S.)

Mr. Bach Comes to Call

Parents' Choice Gold Award (U.S.), American Library Association Notable Children's Recording Award, Parents' Choice Classic Award (U.S.), Practical Home Schooling Reader Award Music Curriculum Category and Educational Audio Cassette Category (U.S.), Film Advisory Board Award of Excellence (U.S.), Certified Gold Record (Canada), Certified Platinum Record (Canada)

Tchaikovsky Discovers America

AUDIO: Juno Award Best Children's Recording (Canada), American Library Association Notable Children's Recording Award, Parents' Choice Classic Award (U.S.), Practical Home Schooling Reader Award Music Curriculum Category and Educational Audio Cassette Category (U.S.), Audio File Earphones Award of Excellence (U.S.), Certified Gold Record (Canada)

BOOK: Canadian Children's Book Centre Our Choice Recommendation, Gibbon Award Finalist Illustration (Canada)

Mozart's Magic Fantasy

Juno Award Best Children's Recording (Canada), Parents' Choice Gold Award, American Library Association Notable Children's Recording Award, Parents' Choice Classic Award (U.S.), Practical Home Schooling Reader Award Music Curriculum Category and Educational Audio Cassette Category (U.S.), Film Advisory Board Award of Excellence (U.S.), Certified Gold Record (Canada), Certified Platinum Record (Canada)

Vivaldi's Ring of Mystery

Juno Award Best Children's Recording (Canada), Parent's Choice Gold Award (U.S.), American Library Association Notable Children's Recording Award, Parents' Choice Classic Award (U.S.), Practical Home Schooling Reader Award Music Curriculum Category and Educational Audio Cassette Category (U.S.), Audio File Earphones Award of Excellence (U.S.), Film Advisory Board Award of Excellence (U.S.), Certified Gold Recording (Canada)

Daydreams & Lullabies

Film Advisory Board Award of Excellence (U.S.), Practical Home Schooling Reader Award Music Curriculum Category and Educational Audio Cassette Category (U.S.)

Hallelujah Handel!

Parent's Choice Gold Award (U.S.), Film Advisory Board Award of Excellence (U.S.), Practical Home Schooling Reader Award Music Curriculum Category and Educational Audio Cassette Category (U.S.)

Educational Awards

Curriculum Administrator Top 100 Districts' Choice Award, Learning Magazine – Teacher's Choice Award, Practical Home Schooling Association Notable Children's Recordings

The Classroom Collection

Teacher's Choice Award Learning Magazine

Susan Hammond, Classical Kids Producer

The Order of Canada for her contribution to arts and education in Canada